Index

Introduction:

The Power of Action in Business

In the world of business, success isn't solely about having the best strategy. While a solid plan is essential, it's **action** that drives results. The truth is, business success is **80% action and only 20% strategy**. Too many business owners fall into the trap of perfecting their strategy, endlessly tweaking plans, and waiting for the "right moment." But here's the hard truth: **without action, all the strategy in the world is meaningless**. It's the work you do, the decisions you make, and the steps you take that bring your ideas to life and propel your business forward.

This book is about helping you understand that it's the **consistent execution** of your vision that leads to real, measurable success. When you focus more on **doing** than on **planning**, you create momentum. That momentum eventually leads to the growth and outcomes you're seeking in your business.

Why Business Owners Struggle

It's easy to get trapped in the planning phase. As business owners, we often convince ourselves that we need more time to refine our strategy, research our market, or perfect the product before we act. But this cycle of overthinking, **analysis paralysis**, and striving for perfect plans is one of the biggest obstacles to business growth.

We've all been there. You spend hours—sometimes days—mapping out the perfect marketing strategy, designing the perfect product, or crafting the perfect sales pitch, yet you never put any of it into action. As a result, your business stagnates. You might find yourself procrastinating, thinking that you need just one more tweak to your plan before it's perfect. But here's the reality: **action trumps perfection.**

In the business world, it's easy to believe that without a perfectly detailed plan, you'll be doomed to fail. But the truth is, **strategy without action is just an idea. Action, on the other hand, leads to learning, growth, and valuable feedback**, allowing you to improve your approach as you go. Every action you take teaches you something about what works and what doesn't, and that real-world feedback is what ultimately helps you build a successful business.

Purpose of the Book

The purpose of this book is simple: to show you how prioritizing **action over planning** can accelerate your business growth, create momentum, and lead to long-term success. We're going to explore how focusing on taking consistent, imperfect action will keep you moving forward, even when the path ahead is unclear.

Throughout this book, you'll learn that **action is the catalyst for success**. You'll discover how **starting before you're ready, taking risks, and learning from your failures** will propel your business far faster than any perfect strategy ever could. By the end, you'll understand that the key to scaling and growing your business lies in how **much you do**, not just in how much you plan.

The goal is not to discredit strategy—it's to help you realize that **strategy without execution is just a dream**. The more you act, the more your business will evolve, adapt, and grow into the successful enterprise you envision.

By prioritizing **execution over endless planning**, you'll break through the barriers that have kept you stuck and accelerate your journey toward success. It's time to stop waiting for the perfect plan and start taking action that moves your business forward.

Chapter 1: The Action-Oriented Business Owner Mindset

The Power of Starting Now

As a business owner, you've probably experienced that constant urge to wait for the "perfect" strategy or the "perfect timing" to launch a new product, enter a new market, or make a big decision. You might feel that if you just spend a little more time researching, tweaking, or planning, you'll be more prepared. But here's the truth: **waiting for perfection is one of the biggest mistakes you can make.**

In business, the **perfect strategy** or **perfect timing** rarely exists. The market changes, customer needs evolve, and unforeseen obstacles will always arise. The longer you wait for the "right moment," the more you delay the growth of your business. **Taking action, even if it's imperfect, is always better than doing nothing**.

It's easy to think that planning and strategy are the keys to success, but without execution, they remain just that—plans. You can plan for weeks or months, but without action, all that preparation is wasted. In fact, the longer you wait to act, the more opportunities you miss.

By starting now—**imperfectly, messily, and without all the answers**—you'll not only gain momentum but also start learning and adapting. Every step, even if it's small, moves you closer to your goals. And as you take action, you'll begin to see where adjustments are needed and where improvements can be made. This is the power of starting now: it moves you out of your head and into the real world, where things actually happen.

Action Over Perfection

One of the most paralyzing myths in business is the idea of the "perfect plan." Many business owners spend endless hours refining their strategy, trying to perfect every detail before taking the leap. They believe that **if the plan isn't flawless, they'll fail**. The truth is, this mindset can be incredibly detrimental to business growth.

Perfectionism kills progress. While it's important to have a roadmap, **a perfect plan doesn't exist because the market and circumstances are always changing**. The idea that you must have everything figured out before you take action is a recipe for inaction. It breeds indecision and stalls growth.

Instead of striving for perfection, start with what you have. **Launch that product, send that email, try that marketing campaign, or test that idea**. You don't need all the answers right now, and you definitely don't need to have everything perfect. Start with a rough idea or prototype, and adjust as you go.

The best business owners know that **perfection is an illusion**, and they embrace the process of continuous improvement through action. It's much better to start with something imperfect and refine it over time based on real feedback than to wait and miss out on opportunities.

Growth Through Action

One of the most powerful things about taking action is that it creates momentum. When you take consistent action, **you build a cycle of progress**—each small action leads to more action, which compounds over time. Momentum is a game-changer in business: it builds confidence, helps you learn from mistakes, and brings tangible results.

Taking action isn't just about doing more; it's about creating opportunities to **learn and grow**. When you act, you begin to see what works and what doesn't. You learn from customer feedback, from the performance of your marketing campaigns, and from the challenges you face. This **real-world data** allows you to **adjust your strategy and improve your business in a way that theory alone never could**.

The more you do, the clearer your path becomes. Each step leads to new insights, helping you refine your business, discover better ways to reach your customers, and make smarter decisions. **Growth doesn't come from planning—it comes from doing**.

By prioritizing action over perfection, you create an environment where you're constantly evolving and improving. Every action you take—whether it's a success or failure—brings you one step closer to your business goals.

In short, **action fuels progress**, and progress is the only way to achieve growth. The more you act, the faster your business will move forward. So, start today, take that first step, and build the momentum that will carry you toward success.

Chapter 2: Why Strategy is Only 20%—Action Drives Results

Understanding the 80/20 Rule in Business

In business, one of the most powerful concepts you can grasp is the **80/20 rule**, also known as the **Pareto Principle**. This rule states that 80% of your results come from just 20% of your efforts. While many business owners focus heavily on strategy, the truth is that only **20% of your time spent on strategy** is enough to provide you with a clear framework for decision-making and direction. The remaining **80%** comes from executing that strategy.

Think about it: no matter how detailed or thorough your strategy is, it will only yield results if you take consistent action. Planning and strategizing lay the foundation, but **execution** is what actually builds the business. Without the 80% dedicated to taking action, your well-thought-out strategy remains just a concept.

In practice, this means that while you should absolutely have a plan, you should **spend the majority of your time** implementing it—adjusting, learning, and improving along the way. Action is the fuel that powers your strategy and drives you closer to success. The most successful businesses are often the ones that prioritize execution over perfection in their strategic planning.

Strategy vs. Execution in Business

In the world of business, strategy without execution is nothing more than an idea—it's a vision that never becomes reality. While strategy provides the framework for where you want to go and how you'll get there, **it's the execution that brings the plan to life**.

Take the example of companies like **Apple** or **Amazon**—while their founders may have started with a solid strategy, it was their ability to **execute that strategy** effectively and adapt as they went along that led to their explosive success. Apple didn't thrive because it had a flawless plan from the start; it succeeded because it continually acted on its vision, testing products, learning from feedback, and improving. Similarly, Amazon grew not because it had the perfect business model from day one, but because Jeff Bezos was willing to take action, experiment, and pivot based on real-world data.

This highlights the importance of execution. A great strategy may look good on paper, but **without constant action**—whether it's launching a product, marketing to customers, or improving operations—it remains just a plan.

Execution drives results because it forces you to **learn from the market** and from your mistakes. While the plan is necessary, without the grit and determination to execute, even the best strategy will fail.

What Action Looks Like in Business

Taking action in business isn't about being busy—it's about moving forward in tangible, result-driven ways. **Action in business means making real moves**, taking calculated risks, and being willing to fail and pivot as necessary. It's about **testing ideas**, **learning from feedback**, and **adjusting your approach** based on what's actually happening in the market, not just in your head.

For example, **launching products** is one of the most direct forms of action. You can't know if a product will succeed until it's out there in front of customers. Testing marketing campaigns, acquiring customers, and even taking risks are all part of the process. While you may have a strategy for how to position your product or what customer demographic to target, **the only way to know if it works is to test it** and **adjust as you go**.

Real-world action also means being willing to pivot. When things don't go according to plan, the ability to adjust quickly is crucial. It's easy to get stuck in your head with the **perfect plan**, but in business, **flexibility and quick adaptation** are essential. What's working today might not work tomorrow, and the businesses that thrive are the ones willing to act and **change direction** when necessary.

In short, action is the key to progress. Without it, your strategy remains theoretical. With it, your business transforms. Execution is where the magic happens, and every step you take moves you closer to your goals. Whether it's launching a new product, refining a marketing campaign, or learning from customer feedback, **action is what drives business success.**

Chapter 3: The Momentum Effect: How Action Creates Business Growth

The Power of Consistency

One of the most powerful forces driving business growth is **consistency**. When you commit to taking small, consistent actions every day, you create momentum that will propel your business forward. While big leaps are exciting, it's the steady, daily grind that produces lasting results.

As a business owner, it can be tempting to focus on big projects or dream about future successes. However, it's the **small, incremental actions** you take every day that will add up to significant growth over time. Whether it's reaching out to a new potential client, optimizing a website, or tweaking a marketing campaign, each consistent action is like laying a brick in the foundation of your business.

Consistency breeds progress. When you focus on daily actions, you develop a rhythm. **Momentum builds**, and before you know it, the small efforts you put in begin to compound into bigger results. The power of consistency lies in its ability to compound—each action not only leads to immediate results but also sets the stage for bigger opportunities in the future.

In business, **success doesn't happen overnight**. But with consistent action, you will start to see the benefits accumulate. Every small step you take today is one step closer to the growth you desire tomorrow.

Breaking Through Inertia

Getting started is often the hardest part of business growth. The initial inertia, that feeling of being stuck or unsure of where to begin, can feel paralyzing. Many business owners spend so much time **overthinking**, trying to plan every step, that they never actually take the first move. The truth is, **the hardest part is overcoming the inertia of doing nothing**.

Once you push through that initial resistance and take action, the process becomes easier. The key to breaking through inertia is to commit to **just starting**, even if it's a small action. It doesn't matter if your first step isn't perfect. What matters is that **you move forward**. The moment you take that first action, the momentum begins to build. From there, you can refine your approach, make adjustments, and scale up, but you can't get to that point until you take the first step.

This is true for almost every aspect of business—from launching a product, starting a marketing campaign, or reaching out to customers. The resistance you feel is normal, but **you must overcome it by simply taking action**. Once you start moving, things begin to flow more naturally, and you'll find it easier to continue.

The Compound Effect of Action

One of the most powerful results of consistent action is the **compound effect**. Just as small actions build momentum, **those actions add up over time** to create exponential growth. What may seem like small, insignificant steps at first will eventually lead to massive outcomes in revenue, customer acquisition, and market positioning.

For example, let's say you dedicate just 30 minutes a day to outreach or follow-up calls. At first, this may seem like a small effort, but over the course of a month or year, those 30 minutes add up to hours of engagement, potentially leading to new clients, stronger relationships, and bigger business opportunities. The more consistent you are with your actions, the greater the returns you will see.

The compound effect also works in terms of learning and refinement. As you continue to take action, you'll gather more data, feedback, and insights. **Each action is a chance to learn**—to improve your products, services, and customer experience. The longer you keep taking action, the better your results become, because you've continuously honed your strategy based on real-world feedback.

This compounding effect is the secret to **sustained business growth**. The more you act, the more results you get. And those results lead to new opportunities, which lead to more action, which brings even bigger results. **Action doesn't just generate short-term results—it multiplies over time, creating a cycle of growth**.

In summary, **action is the key to unlocking business growth**. The consistent effort you put in today will pay off in ways you can't always predict, but you can be sure that over time, your business will be far ahead of where it would have been if you had remained stuck in planning or waiting for the perfect moment.

Chapter 4: Imperfect Action is Better Than Perfect Inaction

The Pitfalls of Perfectionism in Business

One of the most common obstacles business owners face is the pursuit of **perfection**. Whether it's perfecting a strategy, finalizing a product, or crafting the ideal marketing campaign, many entrepreneurs get stuck in a cycle of overthinking and refining. This desire for perfection can become a major barrier to growth, because **no business is built on flawless plans or products**.

The truth is, perfectionism leads to **inaction**. Business owners often spend weeks, months, or even years perfecting every detail before taking the first step. They want the product to be perfect before it hits the market, the strategy to be flawless before execution, or the campaign to be impeccable before launching. But in doing so, they miss out on valuable opportunities for **real-world feedback** and the chance to learn from action.

In the world of business, **imperfection is not a hindrance—it's an opportunity**. It's through action, even if it's imperfect, that you begin to see what works and what doesn't. It's better to have a product in the hands of your customers that isn't perfect, than to have a perfect product that's never seen by anyone. Progress only happens through **doing**, not through perfecting something in isolation. The pursuit of perfection can paralyze your decision-making and cause you to miss out on the momentum that action can create.

Taking Calculated Risks

In business, waiting for the "perfect conditions" to act often leads to missed opportunities. The reality is that **perfect conditions rarely exist**, and even when they do, they often don't last. The true growth happens when you embrace calculated risks and take action despite uncertainty.

Imperfect action is inherently risky—but that's what makes it valuable. When you take action, you begin to gather real-world data and experience that **refines your judgment** and **sharpens your instincts**. Each action, whether it results in success or failure, teaches you something. Perfect conditions won't teach you nearly as much as the lessons you learn from stepping out of your comfort zone.

Risk-taking in business isn't about blind, reckless decisions. It's about weighing the potential outcomes and acting anyway. **Calculated risks** allow you to move forward with confidence, knowing that you can adjust if things don't go as planned. Imperfect action is essential because it forces you to engage with the real challenges of your business. **It's through action and risk that you uncover new opportunities**, refine your strategy, and discover the paths that will lead to success.

Refining Through Action

One of the most powerful benefits of taking imperfect action is that it allows you to **refine your business model** and strategy over time. The more you act, the more you **learn**. Even the best-laid plans will encounter unforeseen obstacles, but each challenge presents an opportunity for growth. By continuously taking action, you get the chance to tweak and adjust your approach based on **actual feedback** rather than theoretical assumptions.

For example, instead of perfecting your marketing strategy for months, launch a smaller campaign, analyze the results, and adjust from there. **The feedback you receive from real customers is invaluable** and will help you make decisions that are far more aligned with the market than any theory could. You can only **refine your strategy through continuous action**, not by waiting for the perfect moment or the perfect plan.

Each step you take, no matter how imperfect, gives you clarity and direction. Over time, the road ahead becomes much clearer. What might have seemed like a complicated or uncertain path in the beginning will reveal itself as a series of smaller, manageable steps. The more you act, the more the path to success reveals itself, and the more you learn about your business, your customers, and the market.

Imperfect action accelerates the process of learning and refining. It's through action that you gain the insights needed to make better decisions and move forward with confidence. The longer you wait for perfection, the longer it will take for you to get to where you want to go.

Refining your business strategy through continuous action is the key to steady growth and long-term success.

Chapter 5: Prioritize Execution, Not Planning

When Planning Becomes Procrastination

Many business owners fall into the trap of over-planning, thinking that the more time they spend crafting the perfect strategy, the more successful their business will be. However, this often becomes a form of **procrastination**. Instead of taking the steps necessary to move the business forward, they stay stuck in the planning phase, tweaking every detail and waiting for the "perfect" time to execute. The problem with over-planning is that it **prevents real progress**.

Planning can be helpful, but when it becomes an endless cycle of refining, rethinking, and adjusting without taking action, it turns into a barrier. **Action is the catalyst for growth**—without it, even the best plans are useless. Business owners need to understand that no plan is perfect from the start, and no amount of planning can replace the invaluable insights gained from taking real, imperfect steps. **Action is the only way to move forward**, and once you begin executing, you'll uncover new information that will guide you more effectively than any theoretical plan could.

To overcome the procrastination of planning, business owners must recognize that it's better to take action, learn from the experience, and then adapt, rather than waiting for conditions to be just right. The key is to stop perfecting the plan and **start executing**—that's where true progress and growth happen.

Execution-First, Strategy-Following

In business, the ideal approach is to prioritize **execution first**, and let your strategy evolve as you go. Action isn't just about implementing a pre-conceived plan—it's about **learning and adapting** based on the results of your efforts. When you begin executing, you'll quickly see what works and what doesn't. This real-time feedback helps you adjust your strategy to be more effective and aligned with the market's needs.

The best entrepreneurs are those who **take action and refine their strategy based on real-world data** rather than guessing or assuming what will work. For example, if you're launching a new product, you don't have to wait for the perfect marketing campaign or branding strategy. You can start by putting the product in front of customers, testing it, gathering feedback, and **improving it based on their reactions**. This kind of **action-first approach** allows you to fine-tune your strategy and adapt it to what actually resonates with your target audience.

By prioritizing execution, you stop waiting for the "perfect" plan and instead focus on creating **momentum through action**. Each step you take provides clarity, and with each failure or success, your strategy becomes sharper. The best part is that this approach accelerates your growth, since you're learning from actual performance rather than hypothetical situations.

Real-World Examples

Real-world examples of successful entrepreneurs who prioritized execution over planning show how powerful action can be in driving results. For instance, **Elon Musk** didn't wait for his rockets to be perfect before launching them. He took bold, calculated steps with SpaceX, launching rockets with imperfections, learning from each failure, and improving his designs. Through constant iteration and a relentless focus on **execution**, SpaceX became a leader in private space exploration.

Another example is **Sarah Blakely**, the founder of Spanx. Rather than waiting for the perfect product or the perfect marketing strategy, she launched her product, marketed it in creative ways, and learned by doing. Blakely refined her approach based on real feedback from customers and her own experiences, eventually growing Spanx into a multi-billion-dollar company. Her success didn't come from perfect planning but from taking action, learning from mistakes, and improving over time.

Patagonia's founder, Yvon Chouinard, is another example of an entrepreneur who took action first. His decision to make environmentally friendly products and improve them along the way helped Patagonia stand out in the crowded outdoor industry. Instead of waiting for a fully polished business plan, Chouinard focused on executing his vision and adapting as the company grew.

These examples show that success doesn't come from waiting for perfect plans or waiting for all the answers to fall into place. It comes from **taking imperfect action**, learning quickly, and **refining your strategy based on real-world experience**. By prioritizing execution and **learning through doing**, business owners position themselves to grow faster and achieve greater success.

Chapter 6: Action is the Fastest Way to Learn and Adapt

The Role of Feedback in Business

In business, the most valuable insights come not from theoretical plans or market assumptions, but from **immediate feedback** generated through action. When business owners take action—whether launching a product, implementing a marketing campaign, or entering a new market—they gain **real-world data** that directly informs their strategy.

Without action, business owners remain stuck in a cycle of **"what ifs"** and **"maybes"**. They might spend endless hours crafting the perfect strategy or imagining ideal scenarios, but without the crucial step of execution, they never know what truly works. Action provides the feedback necessary to validate (or invalidate) assumptions and gives businesses a chance to adjust their approach before they waste time and resources on ineffective strategies.

Immediate feedback is **essential for making informed decisions**. It reveals customer preferences, highlights operational inefficiencies, and uncovers gaps in the market—all insights that can only be obtained through **action**. The longer a business owner waits to act, the longer it takes to gather this data and adjust accordingly.

In short, **action is the fastest way to move from theory to reality**. By acting quickly, even with imperfect plans, business owners can begin collecting feedback that will guide them toward the most effective strategies for success.

Learning by Doing

One of the most powerful ways to learn in business is simply by **doing**. The best strategies, marketing tactics, and product ideas are **shaped by the experience of putting them into practice**. There is no substitute for firsthand experience in understanding what works best for your specific business, industry, and customers.

For example, instead of spending months studying the perfect sales script, the best way to improve your sales process is to start selling. You may make mistakes, but each mistake teaches you something valuable about customer behavior, objections, and the most effective ways to close a deal. As you learn, you can **adjust and refine** your approach, leading to better results over time.

Similarly, marketing strategies are often based on trial and error. A social media campaign might fall flat, but that feedback allows you to **pivot** and adjust your messaging, targeting, or content to align more closely with your audience's preferences. **Real learning happens through action**, not through speculation.

Encourage yourself and your team to embrace the process of **learning by doing**. Taking action and gaining insights from your experiences will allow you to become more agile in responding to customer needs and market shifts. **Every action taken brings you closer to understanding your business better**—and, ultimately, to refining your approach for greater success.

Adjusting Strategy Based on Real Data

Once you start acting and gathering feedback, the next step is to use this **real data** to **adjust and refine your strategy**. The key advantage of action is that it produces results that can be analyzed and used to improve your approach. **Real data from actual customer behavior, sales numbers, and market responses is far more reliable than any theoretical analysis**.

Through action, business owners receive the information they need to make informed decisions. If your marketing campaign didn't perform as expected, you can analyze the data to understand why. Did your message miss the mark? Were you targeting the wrong audience? Or was there a timing issue? The answers to these questions lie in the **data generated by action**.

By continuously adjusting your strategy based on this feedback, you create a **dynamic cycle of improvement**. Each action teaches you something valuable, which you can apply to future decisions. The process of refining your product, marketing, and strategy becomes a continuous loop of learning and adapting that drives your business forward.

The ability to **pivot quickly** and adjust your approach is a key factor in business success. Without taking action and obtaining real feedback, you remain in the dark, unable to improve. However, once you start acting, gathering feedback, and adjusting, you can **fine-tune your business in real-time**, leading to more effective strategies and better results in the long run.

In summary, action is the **fastest and most effective way** to learn what works for your business. By embracing feedback, learning through doing, and adjusting your strategies based on real data, you set yourself up for success and create a business that is agile, adaptable, and primed for growth.

Chapter 7: Overcoming Procrastination and Taking Immediate Action

The Psychology of Procrastination

Procrastination is a common challenge that every business owner faces at some point. Whether it's launching a new product, starting a marketing campaign, or tackling a difficult decision, the **fear of failure**, **uncertainty**, and the desire for **perfection** often keep entrepreneurs stuck in inaction. This emotional resistance to taking the first step can stem from a variety of psychological factors.

Fear of failure is one of the most significant contributors to procrastination. Many business owners fear that their efforts won't be good enough or that their actions will result in failure, so they avoid taking action altogether. This fear creates a mental barrier, paralyzing decision-making and delaying progress.

Another key factor is **uncertainty**. Business owners often hesitate to act because they don't know the outcome in advance. They might not have all the answers or worry that their strategy won't work. The problem is that this hesitation only perpetuates the cycle of **inaction**, preventing them from discovering what actually works.

Lastly, **perfectionism** is a major cause of procrastination. Entrepreneurs sometimes feel the need to have everything perfectly planned out or to launch a perfect product before taking any action. However, the pursuit of perfection often results in long delays and missed opportunities.

The key to overcoming procrastination is realizing that **action itself is the antidote**. The only way to break through these mental barriers is to take the first step, even if it feels imperfect or uncertain. Action builds momentum, and through that momentum, the fear, uncertainty, and perfectionism begin to fade away.

Building the Habit of Action

Developing an action-oriented mindset is crucial for business owners who want to overcome procrastination. It's not about taking big leaps all at once—it's about building the habit of taking consistent, purposeful action. Here are a few strategies to help you build that habit:

1. **Set Clear Goals**: Clear, actionable goals are essential for overcoming procrastination. When you have a specific goal in mind, you can break it down into smaller tasks that are more manageable and easier to execute. This eliminates ambiguity and helps you focus on one step at a time. For example, instead of saying, "I need to grow my business," set a specific goal like, "I will acquire 10 new clients this month."

2. **Break Down Tasks**: One of the biggest reasons people procrastinate is that they see a task as overwhelming. Instead of tackling a massive project all at once, break it down into smaller, actionable tasks. If you're launching a product, your first task might be "create a product page" or "write an email announcement." By focusing on small tasks, the larger project becomes much more manageable.

3. **Commit to a "Start-Now" Attitude**: Commit to taking action immediately, even if it's just a small step. Too often, business owners wait for the perfect moment to start, but the truth is that there will never be a perfect time. Start now, even if it's not perfect, and **you will learn and adjust along the way**.

4. **Focus on Progress, Not Perfection**: Shift your mindset from perfection to progress. Remember that **the goal is forward momentum**—not flawless execution. Taking consistent action, no matter how small, moves you closer to your objective. Every step is a learning opportunity, and even mistakes lead to valuable insights that improve your business.

The One-Minute Rule

One of the simplest yet most effective techniques to overcome procrastination is the **One-Minute Rule**. The rule is simple: commit to working on a task for just **one minute**. It sounds easy, but this small commitment often helps break through the mental resistance to starting. Once you've begun, momentum naturally builds, and you'll often find that you want to continue working beyond that initial minute.

The power of the One-Minute Rule lies in its ability to lower the psychological barrier to action. By making the task feel small and manageable, you're able to bypass the fear of starting. Once you get into motion, it's much easier to continue working on the task, allowing you to build momentum and make progress.

For example, if you're putting off writing an important email or creating a proposal, simply tell yourself, "I will work on this for one minute." After a minute, you'll often find that you're engaged and ready to continue. The One-Minute Rule can be applied to any task, from making phone calls to writing reports, and it's a powerful way to beat procrastination and develop an action-oriented mindset.

Procrastination doesn't have to control your business. By understanding the psychology behind procrastination and taking small, immediate actions, you can overcome the mental roadblocks that hold you back. Building the habit of action is key to transforming your business and creating the momentum necessary for success. Whether it's through setting clear goals, breaking tasks down, or committing to the One-Minute Rule, the important thing is to **start now**. Action will always outpace procrastination—and it's the fastest way to turn your plans into real-world results.

Chapter 8: The Consistency of Action—Key to Long-Term Success

The Importance of Showing Up Every Day

Success in business rarely happens in one big leap. It's the small, consistent actions taken **day after day** that accumulate over time and drive lasting results. Business owners who focus on daily, productive actions are the ones who see growth and success in the long run. Every step forward, no matter how small, contributes to building momentum, learning from mistakes, and making continuous improvements.

Entrepreneurs often become discouraged when they don't see immediate results, but **true success is a marathon, not a sprint**. When you show up every day, even when things seem tough or progress is slow, you are reinforcing the habits that will eventually lead to breakthrough moments. Consistency helps build the foundation for your business's growth, allowing you to adapt and learn through trial and error.

The key to achieving long-term success is making action a non-negotiable part of your routine. **Focus on progress**, not perfection, and trust that each small action you take compounds over time. The magic of business growth lies not in sporadic bursts of effort, but in the **steady, daily grind** of action.

Building Routine and Habits

To turn action into a habit, business owners must structure their day around activities that drive growth. It's about focusing on the tasks that **move the needle**—those that have the most impact on your bottom line, customer acquisition, or operational efficiency. Creating a routine around these high-impact tasks will help ensure that you're consistently working toward your business's goals.

Here's how to build a routine that prioritizes action:

1. **Identify Your Top Priorities**: Start by defining the key actions that will drive your business forward. Whether it's engaging with customers, creating content, improving your product, or networking, knowing what tasks have the greatest impact on growth is crucial. These should be your non-negotiable daily activities.

2. **Create Time Blocks**: Dedicate specific time slots each day for critical tasks. Block out time for actions that require deep focus, such as writing, strategic planning, or working on your product. Also, schedule time for smaller, ongoing tasks like checking emails, customer outreach, and monitoring performance metrics.

3. **Break Large Tasks into Smaller Actions**: Large projects can feel overwhelming and lead to procrastination. Break them down into smaller, actionable steps. For example, if you're planning to launch a new product, set daily tasks such as "finalize the product design," "write product descriptions," or "reach out to suppliers."

4. **Hold Yourself Accountable**: Consistency thrives on accountability. Whether it's through a personal journal, a team, or a mentor, regularly tracking progress helps keep you focused. Celebrate small wins along the way to reinforce the habit of showing up every day.

5. **Limit Distractions**: Make sure your routine is free of unnecessary distractions that can hinder your ability to take consistent action. Create a work environment that promotes focus and efficiency, and set boundaries that protect your time.

Creating a Culture of Action

As a business owner, your actions set the tone for the culture of your company. If you prioritize action, your team will follow suit. Instilling a culture of action within your company is critical to ensuring that everyone is aligned toward execution and progress.

Here's how to build a culture of action:

1. **Lead by Example**: The most effective way to encourage a culture of action is to model it yourself. Be proactive, take calculated risks, and constantly focus on progress. When your team sees you taking action and adjusting as you go, they'll be more inclined to do the same.

2. **Set Clear Expectations**: Encourage your team to embrace a results-driven mindset. Make sure everyone understands their roles and responsibilities in contributing to the

larger business goals. When everyone knows what's expected of them and understands how their actions fit into the bigger picture, they'll feel more motivated to act.

3. **Encourage Experimentation**: A culture of action thrives when employees are encouraged to take risks, try new things, and learn from their mistakes. Give your team the freedom to experiment with new ideas, marketing strategies, or processes. Even if something doesn't work out, the learning that comes from action is invaluable.

4. **Celebrate Progress, Not Perfection**: Reinforce the idea that **progress is more important than perfection**. Recognize and celebrate small wins, efforts, and improvements. This encourages an action-driven mindset and helps your team understand that consistent effort, no matter how imperfect, is more important than waiting for the perfect outcome.

5. **Provide Tools and Resources**: Equip your team with the tools, knowledge, and resources they need to take action. Whether it's access to training, technology, or support from leadership, make sure they have everything they need to execute their tasks effectively. Remove obstacles that might slow down their progress.

By embedding action into your company's DNA, you ensure that your team stays focused on execution, not just planning. As your team starts to adopt a proactive mindset, the collective energy of your business will shift toward constant growth, innovation, and improvement.

Chapter 9: When Action Becomes Adaptation: Pivoting and Evolving Strategy

The Role of Feedback and Adaptation

In business, **action** is not a one-time event but an ongoing process. One of the greatest advantages of taking consistent action is the **real-time feedback** it provides. Rather than waiting for the perfect conditions or a flawless plan, business owners who act quickly are able to gather insights that show them what is working and what needs adjustment.

Feedback can come from many sources: customer responses, sales data, market trends, or even team input. When you continuously take action and remain open to feedback, you develop a **feedback loop** that informs your decisions and helps you evolve your approach. Without action, feedback is non-existent, and decisions become stuck in speculation and theory. Through continuous action, you can adapt and adjust your strategies, products, and operations to stay aligned with market needs, customer expectations, and your own business goals.

Embrace feedback as a critical tool in your strategy. It's not a sign of failure but a valuable resource for improving and refining your business model. Each small action brings new data that drives meaningful changes. **The more you act, the more you learn**—and with each new learning, you refine your business strategy.

Real-Time Strategy Evolution

Strategy is often treated like a fixed blueprint that defines a business's direction. However, in the fast-paced world of business, **strategy is not static**. It evolves with each decision, each customer interaction, and each market shift. The key is to **act first**—take the first step toward your goal—and then **adapt along the way**.

Acting on your plan allows you to test assumptions, validate ideas, and refine your approach based on real-world results. Instead of waiting for the perfect plan or having all the answers, business owners should prioritize execution and adjust their strategies as new insights come in.

Real-time strategy evolution looks like this:

1. **Test Your Hypothesis**: Start with an idea, even if it's imperfect, and launch it. Whether it's a marketing campaign, a product launch, or a new feature, put it into action to see how it performs in the real world.
2. **Gather Insights**: As soon as the action is taken, collect feedback from customers, data, and performance metrics. What did the market respond well to? What needs improvement?
3. **Refine Based on Data**: Use the feedback to adjust your approach, whether it's tweaking the product, adjusting your messaging, or reworking your processes.
4. **Act Again**: Implement the adjustments and test again. This cycle of action, feedback, and adjustment is what drives continuous improvement and keeps your business agile.

By acting first and adjusting later, your strategy becomes a living entity—**one that evolves and adapts** in response to real-world experiences and changing conditions. This evolution doesn't just keep you aligned with your business goals; it also ensures you're continuously improving and refining your approach to meet market demands.

Adjusting Your Approach to Meet Market Demands

The market is constantly shifting, and successful entrepreneurs understand that staying static is a recipe for failure. Strategy cannot be rigid in an ever-changing environment. Instead, it must evolve based on real-time insights gathered through execution.

Execution-driven insights are one of the most powerful tools for adapting to market demands. For example:

- **Product Adjustments**: Through feedback from customers, business owners can refine their products to better meet customer expectations. This might include adding new features, changing design elements, or even pivoting the product entirely.

- **Customer Engagement**: Action helps you understand how your customers interact with your brand. It informs decisions on how to engage with them through social media, content marketing, or customer service. As you act, you can adjust your customer touchpoints to be more relevant and personalized.
- **Marketing Strategy**: Testing marketing campaigns and measuring their performance allows you to see which tactics are driving the best results. Whether it's shifting the messaging, exploring new advertising channels, or adjusting your offers, action provides the data that helps you evolve your marketing strategy.

Successful entrepreneurs constantly adjust their approach based on the data they gather through action. They pivot when necessary, not because their original strategy was flawed, but because **they are committed to finding what works** in real-time. This adaptability helps them meet the demands of a changing market and stay competitive in their industry.

Ultimately, business owners who prioritize action don't just execute a plan—they **evolve their strategies dynamically**. Each step forward generates valuable data that drives continuous refinement, ensuring that their business remains aligned with the ever-changing market and customer needs.

Chapter 10: Success is a Marathon, Not a Sprint—How to Stay Committed to Action

The Long-Term View

In business, success is not an event that occurs in a single moment; it is a journey that unfolds over time. Many business owners, especially those just starting out, expect instant results. However, this expectation can lead to disappointment when progress feels slow or the outcomes don't match the effort put in right away.

It's important to remember that **success is a marathon, not a sprint**. Building a business takes time, and the key to sustained growth is not how fast you can move, but how consistently you can show up and take action every single day. **Staying committed to action**, even when you don't see immediate results, is essential. Each small step you take compounds over time to create significant outcomes.

Business owners must shift their mindset from expecting overnight success to understanding that the true power of growth comes from persistence and **consistent action**. Whether you're building a brand, scaling operations, or acquiring customers, the most successful entrepreneurs are those who keep moving forward, no matter how small the progress may seem. Success comes from **resilience and consistency**, not just quick wins.

Building Resilience Through Action

Every business will face challenges, setbacks, and failures. That's a guarantee. But **action** is the key to developing the **resilience** necessary to overcome these hurdles. When business owners take action, they build a muscle of resilience—each time they make a decision and follow through with it, they grow stronger.

The ability to stay committed to action is what sets successful business owners apart. It's easy to get discouraged when things don't go according to plan, but those who remain focused on action have the ability to bounce back faster. **Action helps you recover** from failures because it forces you to keep moving, to adjust, and to keep learning.

When things don't go well, instead of retreating into doubt, continue taking small, purposeful steps. The faster you act, the quicker you'll discover what needs to change, and the faster you'll be able to adapt and push forward. Action doesn't just create results—it builds mental strength and a mindset of resilience that fuels long-term success.

Celebrating Small Wins

While staying committed to action is key to long-term success, it's also important to celebrate the small wins along the way. In the pursuit of big goals, business owners often overlook the significance of small victories. However, these wins—whether it's securing a new client, hitting a revenue milestone, or receiving positive feedback—should be celebrated.

Acknowledging and celebrating small wins does several things:

- **Boosts Motivation**: Small victories provide the energy and motivation needed to continue pushing forward. Recognizing your progress keeps your momentum alive and combats burnout.
- **Maintains Focus**: Celebrating wins keeps business owners focused on what's working. It allows them to reflect on positive outcomes, which fuels confidence in their approach.
- **Reinforces Commitment**: Every small win is proof that your actions are paying off. It reminds you that the consistent effort you're putting in is leading to tangible results, even if they're not always immediately huge.

Taking time to reflect on your progress and reward yourself for small successes keeps the journey enjoyable and sustainable. It reaffirms the idea that success isn't just about the destination—it's about staying in motion and appreciating the growth you're achieving each day.

As you continue on your entrepreneurial journey, remember that the road to success requires a long-term view, resilience, and a celebration of the small victories. **Commit to taking consistent action** and understand that the rewards come from the accumulation of effort over time. Stay patient, stay resilient, and enjoy the journey.

Final Thoughts

Taking Action is the Key to Unlocking Business Success

As we've explored throughout this book, **action is the cornerstone of business success**. Too often, business owners get bogged down in endless planning, strategizing, and waiting for the "perfect" moment to take action. However, the reality is that **business success is 80% action**. Strategy plays a role, but it's execution that propels growth, drives results, and unlocks potential.

To truly succeed, **you must prioritize action over perfection**. Strategy will evolve as you go—through real-world feedback, trial and error, and continuous execution. The more you act, the clearer your path becomes. Momentum builds with every step you take, and success is the result of those daily, consistent actions. The more you execute, the more your strategy will adapt and improve, ensuring your business keeps progressing.

Remember, it's not about waiting for the perfect plan or perfect timing. **Action is what separates the dreamers from the doers.** The sooner you start, the faster you'll reach your goals. Strategy will follow—naturally, as a result of your experience in the field, and your ability to learn, adapt, and grow.

Your Call to Action

Now that you've read this book, it's time to **stop planning and start doing**. **Take immediate action** in your business today—whether it's launching a product, initiating a new marketing campaign, reaching out to new customers, or refining a current process. Don't wait for everything to be perfect or for the "right" conditions. The only thing standing between you and the success you desire is **action**.

Commit to **starting today**. Whether it's a small step or a big leap, it doesn't matter. The important thing is to move forward and take decisive action. Don't let procrastination, perfectionism, or overthinking hold you back. **Make the decision to act now**, and you'll start seeing momentum build in your business.

Final Words of Motivation

Remember, **action is the only thing standing between you and your business goals**. Strategy, planning, and research have their place—but nothing will move your business forward like taking action. It's not about waiting for the perfect conditions, the perfect idea, or the perfect moment. The sooner you act, the sooner you'll see success.

Business owners who succeed are the ones who take that first step, despite fear, doubt, or uncertainty. They keep moving forward, learning from their mistakes, and improving as they go. **You are capable of doing the same.** Trust in your ability to act, to adjust, and to grow. Your business success is within your reach—and it starts with you taking action right now.

So, what are you waiting for? **Start today, and let your actions create the success you deserve.**

Actionable Exercises for Business Owners - The TL;DR of this Book.

To help you immediately put the principles of action into practice, each chapter concludes with an exercise to apply what you've learned. These exercises are designed to move you out of the planning phase and into action—where real business growth happens. Remember, the goal is progress, not perfection. Each exercise is an opportunity to make a real difference in your business today.

Chapter 1: The Action-Oriented Business Owner Mindset

Exercise: Identify Your First Action

- Write down one specific area in your business where you've been overthinking and hesitating. It could be launching a product, making a sales call, or putting a new marketing strategy into action.
- Commit to taking your first step today—no matter how small. Break down the action into manageable pieces if needed. For example, if launching a product feels overwhelming, focus on setting up the product page or drafting a promotional email.

Chapter 2: Why Strategy is Only 20%—Action Drives Results

Exercise: Create an 80/20 Action Plan

- Identify one area where your business is over-planned and under-executed. Then, for the next 30 days, commit to spending 80% of your time focused on executing, rather than planning.
- Write down your action steps for the next month—be specific about what you're going to do and when. Remember, the key is execution, not perfection.

Chapter 3: The Momentum Effect: How Action Creates Business Growth

Exercise: Implement Daily Action Rituals

- Choose one small task you can do every day that directly impacts your business, such as posting on social media, following up with leads, or reaching out to potential partners.
- Set aside 15-20 minutes each day to focus only on that task. Watch how consistency builds momentum over time.

Chapter 4: Imperfect Action is Better Than Perfect Inaction

Exercise: Take a "Flawed" Action

- Choose a task that you've been holding off on because it needs to be "perfect." Launch a product, send out an email, or share an idea with your team—whatever feels uncomfortable due to imperfection.
- Do it anyway. Allow yourself to be okay with imperfection and see what results you get. Learn from the experience and refine as you go.

Chapter 5: Prioritize Execution, Not Planning

Exercise: Start Now

- Take a task you've been planning but not acting on and commit to completing it within the next 24 hours. This could be something like finalizing your marketing plan, contacting a potential client, or creating a new product offering.
- Don't overthink it—just act.

Chapter 6: Action is the Fastest Way to Learn and Adapt

Exercise: Rapid Testing

- Choose a marketing campaign or product feature to test. Set a small budget or timeline and execute the test quickly.
- Collect data, analyze results, and adjust your approach. Repeat this process and continuously refine your strategy based on real feedback.

Chapter 7: Overcoming Procrastination and Taking Immediate Action

Exercise: Apply the One-Minute Rule

- Identify a task you've been procrastinating on and commit to working on it for just one minute.
- Use that minute to get started—once you begin, you'll often find the momentum to continue.

Chapter 8: The Consistency of Action—Key to Long-Term Success

Exercise: Track Your Daily Actions

- Create a simple habit tracker to record the actions you're taking each day in your business.
- At the end of the week, review your progress. Note any patterns, successes, or areas for improvement.

Chapter 9: When Action Becomes Adaptation: Pivoting and Evolving Strategy

Exercise: Conduct a Weekly Review

- Set aside time at the end of each week to review the actions you've taken and the results they've produced.
- Based on the feedback and data from your actions, decide if you need to pivot or adjust your strategy.

Chapter 10: Success is a Marathon, Not a Sprint—How to Stay Committed to Action

Exercise: Set Long-Term Action Goals

- Reflect on your business's long-term goals and break them down into smaller, actionable steps.
- Set a target for the next three months, six months, and year, and identify key actions you need to take to reach those goals.

Tools and Resources for Action

To help you take swift, consistent action, here are some tools and resources that can support you in your journey:

1. **Trello or Asana** – Project management tools that allow you to create tasks, set deadlines, and track progress. Use them to break down large goals into actionable steps.
2. **Focus Booster** – A time management tool based on the Pomodoro Technique, helping you stay focused and take consistent action in short bursts.
3. **Grammarly** – A writing assistant that ensures your communication is clear and effective, so you can quickly send emails, proposals, and other business documents without worrying about perfection.
4. **Canva** – A user-friendly design tool for quickly creating promotional materials, social media graphics, and marketing content.
5. **Google Analytics** – Use this tool to get immediate feedback on your marketing efforts, so you can quickly adjust and refine your approach based on real data.
6. **Zapier** – Automate repetitive tasks and connect different apps to streamline your workflow, ensuring you're spending more time taking action and less time on manual processes.

These tools can help make the execution process more efficient and effective, keeping you on track with consistent action.

About the Author.

William Burgess (aka Will Kode) is a highly accomplished marketing executive with over 25 years of experience in web-based advertising, data analysis, and publication marketing. Throughout his career, William has demonstrated a unique ability to innovate and create highly successful marketing strategies that drive business growth. His work has earned numerous awards, and he has generated hundreds of millions of dollars in online revenue for his clients through a diverse array of marketing methods and tactics.

With a deep understanding of the digital marketing landscape, William is known for his expertise in crafting tailored solutions that align with each business's specific needs. His focus is not just on short-term success but on building long-term, sustainable growth through continuous action and strategic execution. This book reflects his philosophy that action, not over-planning, is the key to unlocking true business success.

In addition to his professional achievements, William is deeply committed to his community and personal values. He has been recognized with the Congressional Award for his work with individuals with disabilities, showcasing his passion for making a positive impact beyond the business world. William is a true advocate for helping businesses thrive online, guiding entrepreneurs and companies through the complexities of digital marketing with clarity and precision.

Outside of work, William is a proud husband and father of eight children, balancing the demands of a busy career with a commitment to family. His personal experiences have shaped his belief in the importance of resilience, hard work, and the power of consistent action. With a track record of success in both his professional and personal life, William is passionate about empowering others to take control of their own success and achieve their business goals.

Learn more about me at: https://iamwillkode.com/

Made in the USA
Columbia, SC
06 January 2025

49438530R00015